Praise for The "And" Principle

"Giving permission for life's polarities to co-exist, *The "And" Principle* is a portal to freedom."
— Al Secunda, author of *The 15 Second Principle*

"We are human beings on a spiritual journey, and we are spiritual beings on a human journey. *The "And" Principle* helps us on our inner journey of integration, where the joining of black and white is not grays, but vibrant colors."
— Barry Vissell, MD and Joyce Vissell, RN, Ms, authors of *The Shared Heart, The Heart's Wisdom,* and *Meant To Be*

"*The "And" Principle* is a wonderful invitation to embrace all of who we are both individually and collectively. It helps us to expand beyond the limitations of our language and conditioning."
— J. Tamar Stone, MA, *Voice Dialogue* Facilitator and Trainer, Creator of *Body Dialogue*

"This book contains layers of depth, nuance, and wisdom that will provide inspiration for a lifetime."
— Lilibeth Filgueira, Marriage and Family Therapist

"*The "And" Principle* is amazing and brilliant, and its overall concept is quite simple. I savored each page."
— Elaine Rosenson, Marriage and Family Therapist, Director of the *Valley Voice Dialogue Training Center*, Encino, CA

"Stunning in its clarity and wisdom, *The "And" Principle* is a tender source of guidance and consolation."
— Candace Wheeler, MA, Counselor

"*The "And" Principle*, in a seemingly effortless flow, transported me into my own deep, personal being. I was carried on the wings of its poetry, both simple and sublime."
— Diane Miller, Massage Therapist

The "And" Principle

Also by Bill E. Goldberg

Prose

*Protecting the Diamond, Communication Skills to Create and
Maintain Intimacy in Your Life (CD)*

Poetry

Catch the Current
Be Like the River
The Journey

The "And" Principle

Celebrating Self-Acceptance

Reflections, Poems, and Questions
on Leading an Authentic, Integrated Life

Bill E. Goldberg

Catch the Current Publishing

Publisher's Website
www.catchthecurrentpublishing.com

Cover Illustration © 1994 by Eve Olitsky
Monotype Print altered from the original
with the permission of the artist.
Artist's e-mail: eve.o@earthlink.net

Cover and interior design by Marin Bookworks
www.marinbookworks.com

Printed in the United States of America

ISBN-13: 978-0-9661461-6-5
ISBN-10: 0-9661461-6-6

~~~

Catch the Current Publishing

To the beauty, inspiration,
and wisdom of nature.

Acknowledgments

I would like to acknowledge:

The spirit of life, for without its inspiration *The "And" Principle* would never have been conceived or written; it has been a privilege writing this book and my gratitude is immense;

My spiritual teachers, who revealed to me the depth of my spirit, the importance of community, and the power of service;

Elizabeth Smith, a dear, loving friend, who has seen me through thick and thin and whose suggestions, dedication, and support regarding this book have been indispensable and deeply appreciated;

My dance teachers, who changed my life by showing me the transformational nature of movement;

Gavin Frye, for his generosity of time and ideas. His contribution to this book has been greatly valued;

The musicians and songwriters, who have given joy and a depth of emotion to my life beyond measure;

My mother and father, Joyce and Jerry Goldberg, and my family, for their longstanding care and love, and for all they have given and continue to give;

Richard Swatt, for the history we share and his steady life-long friendship;

Lynelle Goodreau, for her friendship and encouragement of my creative endeavors;

My psychological mentors, for their emotional support and giving me tools to live more effectively; and

The poetic tradition, which has the courage, integrity, and wisdom to honor our humanity as part of our spirituality. This tradition expresses the voice of acceptance and inclusion that means so much to me.

Contents

Introduction

The "And" Principle is about the freedom, power, and love that come from self-awareness and self-acceptance. It takes great courage to honor all aspects of ourselves, especially those that we wish to deny. Yet I have discovered, over many years of searching, that such acceptance has been my only hope of having any real peace and fulfillment in life. *Acknowledging all feelings, selves, and dimensions of our being is The "And" Principle.* It is to me a warm embrace and one of the biggest welcomes I have ever received. It sees the gift in each of our emotions, and recognizes the strength that comes from knowing our inner family of selves. *The "And" Principle* is about being attuned to spiritual energy and the transcendent, while also being honest in regards to the real challenges of being alive. It is a book that deals with living in the light and the darkness, integrating the polarities and paradoxes of existence. In our often fragmented, denial-oriented society, this book is a breath of fresh air.

The "And" Principle is a creative expression that contains reflections, poems, and questions on leading an authentic, integrated life. There are nine chapters, and each one begins with a reflection that presents an overview and context for the poems and questions that follow. The poetry presented here was written over the last ten years. Previously, I was never much interested in poetry. In fact, I didn't like most of it. What I had read, I simply couldn't understand. It took too much effort and I often walked away feeling empty. Yet ten years ago another type of poetry entered my life like an unex-

pected visitor. Its entrance was not part of my plan. It began
with an inspiration that I felt just beneath the surface of my
consciousness. When I sensed its prompting, its invitation, I
found myself taking out paper and pen and just writing. What
came forth I found titillating and full of surprises. At times it
was funny and usually it was full of wisdom. I often felt to be
the witness of a wonderful unfolding process that was much
bigger than me. And as I continued to write more poems, life
began to expose me, through books, to a larger poetic tradition that was unlike the words I had read before. I began to
see that in the literary world a vein of gold existed that contained poems I just couldn't get enough of. They were easy to
understand and penetrated my heart and enlivened my spirit.
I considered this kind of writing to be condensed wisdom.
My hope is that The "And" Principle, along with some of the
books it references (see "Footnotes and Further Explora-
tions"), will serve as a portal for you to enter this textured,
deep, and soulful tradition.

Each chapter then ends with a set of questions to assist you,
the reader, in entering into a conversation with the particular
theme presented. My intention is that these questions will ac-
tively involve you in an exploration of yourself, increase your
self-awareness, and deepen your level of self-acceptance. I love
great questions. I actually collect them. A great question can
act like a seed in your consciousness, which once planted and
cultivated can sprout and offer delicious fruit. If truth be told,
I wrote this book, in part, to retrieve "the lost art of curiosity" through the asking of powerful questions. I am convinced
that asking the right questions is a road to great understanding
and revelation. This "retrieval," while important to learning in

general, is highly applicable to our relationships and our experience of intimacy. I am astonished at how few people are curious about others and ask them questions! My wish is that this book effectively raises this issue, and fosters your desire and ability to be curious about life and fascinated by others.

Before you fully launch into reading this book, I want to briefly share a little about my core philosophy and how *The "And" Principle* relates to it. After many years of psychological and spiritual exploration, my thinking simplified and coalesced around a core philosophy that was revealed to me while spending time in nature. For many years, I had considered nature to be my primary teacher and ultimate sanctuary. My core philosophy came from observing rivers, and followed the adage, "The river that continues flowing is the river that remains clean." Put another way, it was "Keep it all moving." I realized that this movement was the essence of physical, emotional, and relational health, and I saw it evidenced in many ways. Emotional acceptance and expression, communicating effectively, practicing forgiveness, physically moving and breathing deeply, dancing, being creative, taking risks, meditating, and being of service all seemed to create a fluidity and grace in living. They are flowing tributaries that feed this vibrant river. *The "And" Principle* fits in with this philosophy through its inclusive, tolerant, accepting nature. For what we resist persists, and denial and judgment tend to keep us stuck. This principle allows things to be the way they are without pretense, and as we accept our experience, our lives inevitably move and shift.

This philosophy and principle also informs my professional life. I have been a practicing psychotherapist for more than twenty years. And as I have applied this philosophy and principle to my clients, I have seen them move towards empowerment and wholeness. They have become more self-accepting, compassionate, capable of intimacy, adventurous, and self-assertive. As a psychotherapist, I have also dedicated much of my career to children and how they are raised, believing that an ounce of prevention is worth a pound of cure. I have applied *The "And" Principle* to the raising of children and have seen them more easily discover their authenticity, preserve their love, and realize their potential. In this spirit, Chapter Six is entitled "Freedom and Discipline: Parenting from *The "And" Principle*," and is devoted to the sanctity of the parent-child relationship.

This book, then, presents much of what has worked in my life and in the lives of those whom I have had the privilege to help. I suggest as you continue reading that you exercise discretion and try on the ideas and practices that appeal to you. If they work, incorporate them in your life. If they don't, put them to the side. I have often thought that life is more like a scavenger hunt than a banquet table. We find what is useful here and there as we travel this wide world. All that we need is usually not neatly arranged in one place and offered to us. My sincere hope is that on your search here you will find some gold that will in some meaningful way enrich your life and ease your way.

It is my pleasure to welcome you to *The "And" Principle*!

The "And" Principle

1

HEAVEN
and
EARTH

Reflection on

HEAVEN and EARTH

*"My soul can find no staircase to heaven
unless it be through earth's loveliness."*
Michelangelo

The "And" Principle was born partly out of my search for a
community that embraced the light of spirit and honored
our humanity, a community that would lift me into the realm of
the eternal while also addressing issues of emotional injury, human conflict, and healthy sexuality. Throughout my life, I had
experienced that you cannot transcend what you repress, and
that denial breeds all sorts of physical and emotional difficulties. I was not about to forsake my integrity and humanness for
a sense of ungrounded joy. I yearned for a community that was
real and solid, with its roots deeply seated in the earth, and its
sense of possibility open to the heavens.

My search for such a community was often frustrated. Some
were filled with spiritual power yet simplistically advocated being happy all the time. Others faced human suffering but lacked
spiritual inspiration. In my frustration, I fancifully thought of
creating my own community. This community would be called

The *"And"* Spiritual Center. Creativity would be its sacrament. Song and dance would be at its core. There would be no split between spirit and flesh, and the body would be embraced completely. The foundation for this center would be a nature-based spirituality. Our building would be in the wilderness where sermons would often come from the mountains, rivers, and trees. This community would have great respect and reverence for the earth and turn to it for inspiration and guidance. Meditation and stillness would be practiced, transporting us into the clear lake of spirit. Through mindfulness, this center would exemplify "divine ordinariness" bringing the holy into the mundane and heaven down to the earth. Washing the dishes, planting your garden, and listening to a friend would be sacred acts. It would provide classes on issues that concern people, like relationships and intimacy, parenting, and physical health. Realizing that service dignifies a spiritual life, this community would balance self-exploration and personal evolution with volunteerism and dedication to values that go beyond self. Transcending the mind that creates dogma and separation, it would be a place of tolerance for all spiritual and religious paths. It would bring people together, knowing the spirit that unites all.

This unifying spirit is in some traditions referred to as the Self. *The "And" Principle* comes from the point of view that this Self resides within every person. It exists beyond the mind and emotions and is a source of great vitality, serenity, grace, and beauty. To experience the Self is to know love without an object. It is contentment that is independent of outer circumstances. *The "And" Principle* is about how to live from the context of the Self in daily life, while integrating our humanness. This pursuit is a way of celebrating heaven and earth.

HEAVEN AND EARTH

Be rooted in the earth
if you are going to reach for the heavens.

Feel the fecund moist earth between your toes
and be grounded in the practical ways of the world
before you entertain merging with light,
entering subtle realms of mist,
and transcending into oneness.

Knowing separateness makes oneness safe.
The earth supports heaven.
A strong ego allows for glimpses of the divine.

Otherwise your house lacks a foundation,
and a hurricane of light will demolish thin walls.

THE SILVER LINING AND THE CLOUD

He who sees the silver lining
and not the cloud
gets rained upon.

And he who sees the cloud
and not the silver lining
also gets rained upon.

BOTH

Seeds germinate in the darkness
and blossom into the light.

Honor both.

ILLUMINATION

Illumination is like taking a faded rainbow,
brightening and intensifying the colors,
adding some texture.

And then realizing
we are also the light
that moves so beautifully through the prism.

TWO SPIRITUALITIES

Two spiritualities,
one the road less traveled,
one the road more traveled.

The road less traveled
is a wide road that embraces it all,
every season of the heart.
It is a road for the courageous
who have the strength to be with the fullness of life.
Loving the light, embracing the darkness.
Comfortable with joy and accepting anger.
Surrendering to love and able to grieve well.
Knowing the transcendent and navigating with fear.

The road more traveled is a narrow road.
It is really the difficult dance of denial,
not wanting this feeling and pursuing that one.
It's a dance that will leave you tired.
It is a road that embraces heaven but denies the earth,
that talks of love and light but forsakes our humanity.
It is a road taken by those who fear attachment
and are petrified to feel their pain.

AND

There is a place in me that has never been injured,
and there is an injured place in me that I acknowledge
   and respect.

I take responsibility for my life and healing,
and I find hurtful what I experienced when I was vulnerable.

There is a transcendent awareness in me that exists beyond
   time and space,
and I experience temporality living in the world.

I celebrate my spirit,
and I embrace my thoughts and feelings.

I pray for guidance,
and I take initiative and act in my life.

"Either or" is half the truth.
"And" honors me completely.

IF IT ISN'T HERE, IT ISN'T ANYWHERE

If it isn't here,
it isn't anywhere.

If it isn't watching your child go into peals of laughter,
if it isn't letting the taste of chocolate linger on your tongue,
if it isn't watching the sky change color inviting in the night,
it isn't anywhere.

If it isn't enjoying the silhouetted tree against the sky,
if it isn't feeling the comfort of a warm embrace,
if it isn't seeing innocence in a baby's face,
it isn't anywhere.

What is right before us
contains all the beauty,
mystery, and majesty
that we'll ever need.

A BEAUTIFUL PLACE

The birds frolicked in the sky
like little children playing.

The sunlight filtered through the trees
with a scintillating beauty.

The mountains surrounded me
releasing my heart.

I took another step on soft soil
just feeling good in a beautiful place.

CHAPTER 1 – QUESTIONS TO PONDER

1. What are some of the most courageous choices you've made that exemplify the road less traveled?

2. If you could grant yourself two prayers to be answered, what would they be?

3. Describe several of your most cherished spiritual experiences.

   How did they change your life?

4. Reflect on your connection to nature and the earth.

   How does this connection affect your life?

   What are the qualities of nature you most appreciate?

5. How does your spiritual or religious orientation view your humanness, including your emotions, sexuality, and challenges?

   Is your humanness to be embraced, transcended, rejected...?

6. What is sacred to you, and why?

EXPANSION and CONTRACTION:

Honoring Emotional Integrity

Reflection on

EXPANSION and CONTRACTION:

Honoring
Emotional Integrity

By the time I was eighteen, I felt very little.
It took many years and much hard work to rediscover my
feelings. This chapter is dedicated to all children that they
might not have to endure such a struggle.

Bill E. Goldberg

From an emotional perspective, much of western culture is in a fallen state. We have divorced ourselves from our bodies, feelings, and instincts and sought refuge in a mental cathedral that has a wobbling foundation. Emotional intelligence is a scarce commodity. *To meet people who feel secure within themselves, are comfortable with all their emotions, and can effectively navigate the world of relationships, is rare indeed.*

Emotional integrity is the ability to feel and appropriately express all feelings. The full spectrum of our emotions is embraced just as we would accept all the colors of a rainbow. If one color were excluded, the rainbow would be missing a part of itself. Emotional integrity can also be compared to accepting the four seasons. Winter, spring, summer, and fall each have their own rhythm and beauty as does each of our emotions. And as natural as the seasons are, so are the seasons of our hearts.

Accepting emotions is crucial to mental and physical health. Denying them can agitate the mind and wreak havoc on the body. Repressing anger, pain, love, fear, and delight is like fighting ocean waves. It leaves you tired, confused, anxious, and depressed. *Our choice is between the anxiety and depression that come from emotional denial, and the aliveness, vulnerability, and intimacy that are made possible through emotional integrity.*

Emotional denial can take many forms. It can take the form of working long hours and going numb in the process, or in staying so busy we distract ourselves from our inner life. It can take the form of adopting a way of thinking or a philosophy that denies our humanness. Rationalization, over-intellectualization (thinking too much), and repression are also forms of emotional denial. We may abuse drugs and alcohol, overeat, and engage in excessive sexual activity in order to deny our feelings. All in the name of avoiding pain, we engage in ways of thinking and behaving that are destructive and ultimately cause more pain than the original feelings we are attempting to avoid. Recovery from emotional denial and addictive behaviors is essential to finding fulfillment in life. And recovery will usually involve establishing emotional integrity, discovering our authenticity, and learning how to be close with others.

Breathing, Movement, and Feeling

I have found that working with my body and movement greatly enhances my ability to feel. It is through breathing and opening my body that my emotions deepen, become more fluid, and can be released. It is from the celebration of dance and sweat, sinew and bone, from leaving my mind and entering the beat, that I have discovered my entryway to emotional vibrancy. For this revelation I am grateful, as the ability to feel has saved me, simplified my life, and allowed me to experience deeper intimacy with myself and others.

Honoring Expansion and Contraction

Anxiety and depression are forms of contraction, whereas emotional acceptance and expression are forms of expansion. And even though the former are contracted, they are to be honored and often bring with them many gifts. Anxiety, for example, can lead you on a journey towards accepting all of your feelings. In therapy, I have seen clients' anxiety levels motivate them to develop emotional integrity. As they allow themselves to feel, especially anger and sadness, their anxiety lessens. Depression that is being caused by leading an inauthentic life can lead you to a more purposeful vital existence. Life is a school, and our suffering often leads us to learn valuable lessons.

We need to come back to nature. We are born with tear glands. We are born with adrenalin which can save our lives when we're cut off in traffic. We can learn a lot about what's natural from observing young children. We see fresh, open beings with wills as strong as steel. They know what they want and what they feel. They are truly emotionally alive, able to feel fully. *It is time to cooperate with life.* Part of this cooperation is developing emotional integrity.

The Complexity of Our Emotions

Whereas accepting our emotions can be important for our health, it is essential that we discriminate between the healthy acceptance of emotions and the destructive creation of feelings. The following three questions will assist us in distinguishing between these two types of emotions:

Fluid Feelings

1. Are you able to feel and release your feelings or are you holding on to them?

   Whereas we want to accept and celebrate our emotions, we don't want to hold on to them. We want to feel them, let them go, and return to the Self. Our emotions are like waves, the Self is like the ocean. Feel, flow, be natural with your emotions, and keep coming back to the ocean. This constitutes a graceful life and is freedom.

Rationally-Based Feelings

2. Are your feelings created by rational or irrational thoughts?

   The concept of emotional integrity discourages feeding emotions that are based on irrational thoughts. Self-inquiry becomes important when discriminating between these two types of feelings. A careful examination of the thoughts that create many of our emotions is part of this inquiry. Examples of emotions that are created by irrational thoughts are the fear or sadness that results from catastrophizing or jumping to irrational conclusions.[1]

Present Feelings

3. Are your feelings an appropriate response to a present situation or are they the result of an unfinished, unresolved circumstance from your past?

   For example, you are giving a speech and become anxious because you think that certain people in the audience are being critical. In fact, they are not. You are merely thinking that they are because you were raised with a lot of judgment. Encouraging your anxiety in this situation would be inappropriate.

If upon reflection, you realize that many of your emotions are not fluid, rationally-based, or present, I still suggest that you allow them and treat them with respect. Find out what you need to learn from them, what needs to shift in your awareness. Then, as with all feelings, let them go, and return to the Self.

So, whereas *The "And" Principle* acknowledges all feelings and learns from every aspect of living, it does not *encourage* all feelings and give carte blanche for you to do whatever you want. It is a *principle of discretion* that distinguishes between healthy and unhealthy ways of dealing with emotions, and the constructive and destructive ways of acting in the world. It is a *value-based principle* that recognizes the complexity of life, the conflicting interests within and between people, and the need for *compromise* to create a harmonious existence.

Welcome to the human predicament! Sorry, I wish it were simpler. As Thomas Moore said in his book, *Original Self,* "Live simply, but be complicated." [2]

JUST BELOW THE SURFACE

I awoke one morning depressed and numb.
I put on some music and began to dance
and a river of tears flooded my heart.

Oh, what resides just below the surface.

SELF-EXPRESSION

Weeds break through
asphalt and concrete
to feel the sun,
and the pulsations
within a human being
have the same tenacity
for self-expression.

FALLING TOGETHER

You cry,
and people say, "You are falling apart."

What is this?
The fall of humanity in the Garden of Eden?

We have become estranged from ourselves.

Is it falling apart when the rain comes in winter?
Is it falling apart when the wind blows or lightning strikes?
These are natural rhythms of nature.
Parts coming together. Parts that make up *life itself.*

So are your tears.
Your pain is natural.
When you feel it, a beautiful, sacred part of you is falling
    into place.

The next time you feel your pain,
see it as a homecoming,
a falling together,
a gathering of your parts
that make up the strong house in which you live.

CATCH THE CURRENT

Catch the current of your emotions,
it is strong.

Catch the current of your spirit,
it is deep.

Catch the current of your authenticity,
it is powerful.

Catch what is current,
what is present,
it is alive.

HOW I SHINE

How I shine
when I'm in my element,
surrounded by earth,
trees, a lake.

I'm home,
I'm happy,
and I shine.

A RELATIONSHIP WITH YOURSELF

How often have you seen
a person walking down the street alone
laughing out loud?
It's wonderful to have relationship with yourself.

VALUES

Feelings are dear, accept them.
Yet don't always follow their promptings
for they sometimes will lead you to inaction
or into some dark alley of distraction.

Allow your values to enter the conversation.
They are the guideposts that you birthed
in quiet moments of reflection and dreams.
Let your values now mix with your feelings,
shine a light on a path you already have chosen,
and guide you home.

LIFE IS NOT A STRAIGHT SHOT

Up and down
and all around.
Standing tall
falling down.
Feeling divine
feeling maligned.
Triumphant
defeated.
Weak as a lamb
on top of the world.

Cycles
Rhythms
Changes.

Life is not a straight shot.

NATURE IS MY TEACHER

Nature is my teacher,
she contains all moods.
Sky-splitting thunder,
streaking lightning,
cleansing rain,
the stillness of dawn,
the tender warmth of the sun,
soft gentle mist,
powerful winds,
so varied,
so expressive,
teaching me
to embrace it all.

FREEDOM

Welcoming our experience
we accept our emotions,
and watch their play
with utter compassion.

Longing, fear, anger, and grief,
ecstasy and love
appear without judgment,
and we realize that we have become
the allower of all things,
and have finally embraced freedom.

CHAPTER 2 – QUESTIONS TO PONDER

1. How does your experience of nature reflect your wide range of feelings?

2. Which emotions can you easily feel and release, and which do you deny or hold on to?

3. What did your family of origin teach you about emotions? Which were acceptable? Which unacceptable?

4. Describe a time when you felt deeply touched by another's sensitivity.

5. What activities, places, or people bring you great joy? How could you have more pleasure in your life?

6. Breathing and movement often precede feeling. What do you do in your life that assists you in being grounded in your body and feeling your emotions fully (i.e., exercise, walking, playing a musical instrument, dancing, or sexual expression)?

LOVE
and
LOSS

LOVE and LOSS

"Life is the flower for which love is the honey."
Victor Hugo

It is love that brings sweetness into life. It's companionship, sharing the ups and downs, and having someone witness your time here on earth that eases the way. It is coming home to a warm embrace, feeling your cat snuggle close to you when you sleep, or having your child elated just to see you that goes to the center of a well-lived life. These are the moments that are meaningful at journey's end. "How did you love?" becomes the central question when reflecting on the life that you have lived.

Love expresses in different ways. There is interpersonal and transpersonal love. Interpersonal love exists among people and between people and pets. Transpersonal love is the experience of the Self. It exists independent of relationships or circumstance and resides deep in the center of your being. Knowing this place assists you in more fully loving yourself and is the springboard for loving others.

The other side of interpersonal love is loss, for life is change and death is intrinsic to it. *I have often thought that to love another wholeheartedly is life's most courageous act.* As human beings we are so vulnerable, needing love, yet knowing that we will eventually lose all that we hold dear. How can we deal with such huge losses? What can we do with our feelings when we are no longer with someone that we have loved for many years? What could possibly bring life back into balance, into some sort of equilibrium? The answer is to grieve. Grief is a thunderstorm that jolts us to our core. It cracks open the heart and relieves the pressure. After the storm there will be a calm, and hopefully we will feel that the loving enriched our lives and was worth it.

There is no place where emotional integrity is more crucial than in the grieving process. The feelings are so powerful that they must be released to maintain one's physical and mental health. Many people hold back their feelings for fear of being overwhelmed. Others hold back as a way to stay attached to the deceased. *The delicate dance is one of feeling and letting go.* And to be held in someone's arms as we weep is our good fortune.

Some of the greatest blessings of my life have been the people and animals in it. The arenas of friendship, companionship, and romance have been rich and rewarding. I feel fortunate to be surrounded by wonderful, loving, creative people. And while I have felt enriched by relationship, I have also experienced many losses. These have also been important, for they have dug a deeper well in my heart and expanded my ability to love. I connect strongly and value my capacity for intimacy, so certain losses have been particularly difficult. Some of them have wrenched me to my core. Yet suffering from lifelong isolation and loneliness is also wrenching in its own way, and so I have joined the courageous of heart and my arms are open wide.

Kindness

To be fully human is to love from the depth of our hearts and feel our pain when we experience loss. And from that love and grief we can develop compassion and empathy for others, for we all share the same humanity. We all have cried ourselves to sleep at night. The fruit of this compassion is often kindness. A central quality of being fully human is simply to be kind and to take care of one another. Then we can more easily live these beautiful words of poet Naomi Shihab Nye:

KINDNESS (Excerpts)

"Before you know what kindness really is
you must lose things,
feel the future dissolve in a moment
like salt in a weakened broth…

Then it is only kindness that makes any sense anymore,
only kindness that ties your shoes
and sends you out into the day to mail letters
and purchase bread,
only kindness that raises its head
from the crowd of the world to say
It is I you have been looking for,
and then goes with you everywhere
like a shadow or a friend."[3]

THE EQUATION FOR FEELING
LIFE'S WORTHWHILE

Love fully.
Be incredibly vulnerable.
Experience the completeness
of love's pleasure and comfort.

Experience loss.
Let the pain wash over you
like the waves wash over the sand.
Convulse with the pain.
Let it come, let it go,
and eventually it will dissipate.

Then love again,
in your own time.

GRIEF

A reservoir of pain
resides deep in your core.

Let it out.
Let it out.

Only on the other side of grief
is peace.

THESE LITTLE ONES (Our Beloved Pets)

They come to teach us about death...and life.
These little ones come to teach us life's big lessons.
They make their way into our hearts
and we become close beyond imagining.
Then they leave us and we grieve.
And this grief is spirit's catalyst
forcing us into spiritual dimensions,
where we see them once again
as they always were,
realizing that they were just temporarily
camouflaged in fur.

THE HUMAN DRAMA

We are so scared of getting close
and we so need to be close.

Therein lies the human drama.

FOR THE SAKE OF LOVE

Our goal is to take risks
in the presence of fear
for the sake of love.

READY

I can grieve, so I can love.
I can lose, so I can find.

THE BLOSSOMING

The blossoming that comes from love.
Seeing the future in her face.
Seeing a polished stone in a rough cut.
Seeing the flower of the heart
that opens with a gentle touch.
The laughter that comes from acceptance.
The beauty that comes from encouragement.
The spontaneity that comes from safety.

Without love,
you see a fraction of a rigid self.
With tenderness,
you see a lovely sculpture emerge.

The blossoming that comes from love.

SOFT, SWEET TOUCH

I dream about
a time to come,
when I will arise
to the morning sun,
and slowly rise
to the soft, sweet touch
of your face.

PERMISSION TO DISAPPOINT

Permission to disappoint,
freedom of the highest order.
It is saying, "I love you
even when you don't fulfill my needs."
It's a mature loving
not a narcissistic using.
It is a life-giving tree
not a parasitic weed.
Otherwise you are just someone's appendage,
conditionally loved only when you please.

Permission to disappoint,
freedom of the highest order
and love of the deepest kind.

RESONANCE

A feather quivers in the wind
and whispers a gentle sound.

A man quiets,
the spirit speaks.
A baby sighs,
the mother caresses.
A lover tears,
her beloved holds.
A woman's arms open,
the man embraces.
Her eyes invite,
he kisses.

Resonance
Attunement
Congruence
Delight.

CHAPTER 3 – QUESTIONS TO PONDER

1. Remember a time when you were experiencing a special romantic love.

   In what ways does loving bring meaning into your life?

2. How has friendship enriched your life?

3. Reflect upon a deep loss that you've experienced.

   How did your grieving deepen your ability to love?

   How did it develop your compassion for others?

4. In what ways might you maintain distance in a relationship to avoid intimacy (i.e., communicating indirectly, being judgmental, or creating fights)?

5. Have you ever loved someone completely without withholding?

   If yes, what allowed you to be so courageous?

   If no, what has stopped you from being fully committed?

"Memory nourishes the heart,
and grief abates."
Marcel Proust

4

EXPRESSION
and
CONTAINMENT

EXPRESSION and CONTAINMENT

"Everything has rhythm. Everything dances."
Maya Angelou

Expression and containment are two of the great rhythms of life, and they are no more important than in the realm of relationship. Talking and listening, expression and containment usually need to be in balance to have a fulfilling interaction. It is reciprocity, that easy flow back and forth, which makes for a healthy connection. Yet deep listening is a rare phenomenon in the world today. It is the gateway to knowing another. To effectively listen to someone, you must be able to temporarily *forget about yourself*. And that takes discipline and work, for it requires a containment of your own mind that wants to express itself.

When I think of criteria for friendship, I think of someone who can talk, listen, and be spacious. *Being spacious* has to do with having room inside ourselves to take another person into our consciousness. It has to do with giving people time to talk, where we listen and *ask them questions* without talking about ourselves. It has to do with recovering the lost art of curiosity. We watch a movie for hours and take in characters and a plot without saying a word. We need to be able to watch and listen to another person and get to know them as well. Then hopefully the gift of spaciousness will be returned. This constitutes a graceful conversation. So, if you would, imagine for a moment a world where people are concerned with being more inquisitive than right, more flexible than dogmatic, and more interested than interesting. I am certain that such a world would feel safer, be more fun, and encourage a more harmonious, loving way of life.

What Allows for Listening and Spaciousness

So you may ask, "What allows people to listen and be spacious?" I will present four prerequisites.

1. *Openness* – Real listening requires us to be open and receptive. Many people have difficulty being open because they have been emotionally injured in their lives, and have become closed, afraid to let someone else in.

2. *Reasonable Self-Esteem* – Reasonable self-esteem, in part, has to do with feeling secure within oneself. If people are secure within themselves, they do not need to inappropriately interrupt others, try to impress them, or talk too much about themselves. Someone with self-esteem can listen and be spacious, feeling full inside, and not need so much attention. Sometimes, still waters run deep.

3. *Emotional Integrity* – If we can accept our own feelings, we can more easily listen to others. When other people speak, they often express feelings. Their feelings stimulate ours, and if we can't tolerate our own feelings, then we can't listen effectively.

4. *A Quiet or Controllable Mind* – I mentioned earlier that listening is work. It is work because we have to be able to discipline our minds. It is said that the mind is a great slave and a bad master. It is to be valued and respected, and it must know its rightful place. I have a saying, "An untamed mind is much ado about nothing." When the mind knows discipline, it can focus and listen. It becomes a powerful, creative force. This discipline must be practiced. Meditation is one way to do this. It is also in disciplining and purifying the mind that we are able to perceive the Self, which is a source of calm and self-confidence.

Narcissism

Our culture presently is experiencing a disease of epidemic proportions that makes listening very difficult. *The disease is narcissism*, a preoccupation with self, and it is the death knell of intimacy. Notice at a party how few people ask you five questions without talking about themselves. Notice the competitive speech in social interactions, the raised voices, and interruptions. If you become aware that you exhibit these behaviors, please be compassionate with yourself. This is not a call to judgment but to awareness and understanding, and to learn the ways of intimacy.

Self-Expression

When properly balanced with containment, self-expression is crucial to our mental and physical health, and to our effectiveness in the world. Expression in relationship is essential, for communication is what allows love to flourish. Yet for self-expression to be effective, it must be educated. Without effective communication skills, expressing oneself can do more harm than good. Invest in your relationships by learning these skills. Like knowing how to use ropes and pitons in mountain climbing, these skills can save the life of your relationships. For an in-depth guide to communication skills, I refer you to my CD, *Protecting the Diamond.*[4]

Containment and Loving with Discretion

Flowers open and close according to the sun's warmth. With warmth, flowers open; with kindness, the heart opens. When cold comes, the flower closes, and faced with insensitivity, a heart wisely closes for its own protection. One of the main lessons of life is to learn to *love with discretion.* That is, to know with whom we can open with safely, who will receive our feelings with care. We must learn to open and close, express and contain depending on the emotional health of the people we are interacting with. So being a good judge of character and following our intuitive knowing becomes crucial to attracting and developing healthy relationships. I often say to clients, "It is not wise to invite a person with a machine gun into your living room, and it is not wise to invite judgmental people into your heart." I also give clients two criteria before trying to work out problems with others. The requirements are that the other person not be overly defensive, and that he or she think rationally. If someone is overly defensive and thinks in a distorted way, you won't be able to resolve conflict. By attempting resolution you are in essence setting yourself up for frustration, which is not a healthy thing to do. So learning containment and not trying to solve a problem with someone may just be the right choice.

Boundaries

Having strong boundaries is part of containment and expression. It's being able to say "no" to people and feeling good about yourself regardless of their reaction. It is not taking people's reactions to you personally and in essence keeping *their energy contained* and out of your space or your boundary. Having boundaries is crucial in a world filled with so much narcissism. Narcissistic people make the fatal flaw of believing that you are like them, so they give you advice. They think, "If this is good for me, it must be good for you." *Not having strong boundaries in a world full of people who are giving advice is dangerous.* You are unique and what works for someone else may not work for you. Therefore, reserve your sense of critical analysis as you listen to people, filter what they say, and give up your power to no one. This is imperative with the mass proliferation of information via the Internet, television, and other sources. Strong boundaries make your journey on this planet a smoother ride.

In conclusion, enjoy exercising your right to containment and expression. They are your two great prerogatives.

HARMONY

It's like jazz.
The keyboards lead,
center stage.
Soon relinquishing to the bass
who shines with deep tones.
Then making way
for the riffs of the lead guitar,
that finally surrenders to the singer
who bares her soul in song.
Harmony, synergy.
Sharing the stage.
Better together than alone,
they're making beautiful music.

All relationships should be like this.

FLIRTING WITH AVAILABILITY

Some people flirt with bodies.
The allure of the physical
with all its shapes and sizes
curves and scents.

Some flirt with the mind.
Banter, talk, the intrigue of the intellect.

Some flirt with distance.
Sarcasm, arguments, and competition.
The tools of those afraid to get close.

I like to flirt with *availability*.
With those who are present, alive, and spacious.
Who can be in the moment and take me in *fully*.
Who are able to enter a conversation
full of reciprocity.
Willing to surrender, full of trust,
and overflowing with spontaneity.
Playful and looking for fun!
Willing to be real, longing for connection.
Who are open, wide open, and ready.
Ready for love,
the greatest adventure of all.

THE TRUTH IS IN THE CIRCLE

Theory can be dangerous.

Ideas unapplied, unchallenged,
lack foundation, and can be misunderstood.

Truth is revealed when a circle of people
question, confront, and apply ideas to real situations.

The confrontation of ideas
puts flesh on their bones and raises them to life.

WISDOM

Wise people rarely give advice,
they just ask lots of questions.

BOUNDARIES

A beautiful seagull
approached me as I ate my lunch.
I spoke to her sweetly.
I offered her my love
but not my tuna sandwich.

A PREGNANT PAUSE

An oh so pregnant pause,
replete with wisdom
and a full heart,
that knows not competition,
sits in repose in its fullness and listens,
takes me in,
and lets me continue to hold the microphone.

This pause,
this oh so pregnant pause,
gives birth to intimacy,
speaks volumes,
means everything,
means *everything*,
that I'm seen,
valued,
and loved.

RECOVERING THE LOST ART OF CURIOSITY

Become the grand inquisitor.
Ask the great questions of life.
These questions will, like explorers,
lead you to discover the unknown lands of another.
Completely forget yourself for awhile,
and become the curious one.
Your curiosity about others
is like rain to parched land.
Your interest says, "I value you,"
and is more valuable than a diamond ring.
It is the medicine that will heal
the plague of narcissism that has swept our world.
It will usher in the age of the quiet mind,
and bring forth *dynamic dialogues* that will nourish the hungry.
Dialogues that will replace the *monologues* of the emotionally injured,
who became consumed with themselves to stop their bleeding.
No judgment, just unhealthy to be around
and unpleasant to the eye, blood everywhere.
It's time to clean up,
and become the pristine mirrors for our brothers and sisters,
who need reflection to see their beauty.
Undaunted by competitive, loud speech,
(the tools of narcissism),
this stillness of welcoming
is an invitation to the age of listening,
that will heal this planet of potentiality.
A potentiality that manifests through love.
A love that becomes real through connection.
A connection that is born of curiosity.

Become the grand inquisitor.
Your questions are like gold coins
thrown into the wishing well of life.
A well that will birth dreams.

A CLOUD

A cloud,
wispy gas,
can block the mighty sun.
And a hurt feeling,
unresolved,
can block years of loving.

THE GUARDIAN OF LOVE

Sharing feelings
is the guardian of relationship,
the guardian of love.

COMPLETE THE CIRCLE

Appreciations unspoken
leave circles broken.
Artists, poets, and musicians,
family, friends, and lovers
fill this journey with so much beauty.
What would we do without them?
Appreciations spoken
complete circles broken.

CHAPTER 4 – QUESTIONS TO PONDER

1. In what ways does reciprocity characterize your relationships?

   When you are in conversation with others, are you more concerned with being interesting or being interested?

   Do you typically talk more than listen or listen more than talk?

2. Can you remember a time when someone gave you the gift of spaciousness, taking you in with sincere interest and curiosity?

   How did you feel?

3. Can you remember a time when you gave the gift of spaciousness to someone else?

   How did they react? How did you feel?

4. Think of a time when you shared something special with someone and felt disappointed and worse after the sharing.

   What can you learn from this experience?

   What qualities would you want someone to possess before sharing your special experiences with them?

5. How do you respond when others exercise containment and don't want to share something with you?

   Do you respect their privacy or do you take offense?

6. How strong are your boundaries in your relationships?

   Do you lose yourself when around others?

Do you take on other people's pain, opinions, and judgments?

What are some ways you can strengthen your boundaries?

STRENGTH
and
VULNERABILITY

STRENGTH and VULNERABILITY

"Let the gentle bush dig its root deep
and spread upward to split the boulder."
Carl Sandburg

There are few human qualities that are as misunderstood as vulnerability. Our culture sees vulnerability, sensitivity, and being emotional as weakness. "Big boys/girls don't cry," "Real men/women aren't afraid," echo in the annuls of our society. Yet nothing could be further from the truth. Vulnerability is strength, the strength to endure all feelings. It is the courage to be real in the face of loss, to meet the challenges of daily living head on. Strong people can writhe in pain and exult in ecstasy. And knowing their spiritual essence makes this pain bearable, for it doesn't consume them totally. In reality, weakness is fear of our pain, feeling that we aren't strong enough to endure it, that it will annihilate us. I've been in both places, denying it and feeling it. I'll vote for feeling it. I will take grief over anxiety and depression any day. And neither is a picnic.

We fear that exposing our needs will lead to rejection, yet with healthy people the opposite usually occurs. People love to feel needed and when you are in pain, you give your friends a chance to take care of you — a rich experience of the heart. Marriages and friendships are built on such moments.

We need to redefine ourselves and see our vulnerability for what it is: true strength. We need to see our tears as "falling together," not "falling apart." We need to teach our children that all of their feelings and parts are acceptable. And as we deal with our humanness head on, directly, our world will be less confusing. We won't see the destructive consequences of powerful impulses that have been lurking in the dungeons of our being, contorting and distorting themselves, eventually rising up and manifesting in violent, depraved ways.

Strength takes on other forms besides vulnerability. We need to be able to call forth many different selves to live effectively. The warrior is a great self. This shade of strength stands up to the bullies of the world and fights against injustice. It doesn't tolerate abuse and has boundaries. It is tough love, saying "no" and defending itself physically if need be. This part is sassy, not so sensitive, and gets the job done. Warriors suffer wounds, dress them, and carry on. They are into survival, not self-pity. Self-pity in battle would be their demise. Warriors think quickly, are shrewd, and wisely size up their opponents. They are persistent and endure. They have stamina and see the fight to the end.

Strength manifests in business as handling many rejections until the sale occurs. And salespersons mainly get rejections. It's the woman dating who kisses a lot of frogs until the prince arrives. I have thought that life is not for the timid. It's often the tenacious ones who get the prize. I've known many talented, bright people whose lives were not very successful. I have known others, less talented and bright, who have a strength and fortitude that comes from self-confidence. They are often the ones who have created what they want in their lives.

So I invite you to welcome your vulnerability. Its rewards are immeasurable. And be tough and sassy. Bring out your warrior when necessary. And always remember: vulnerability is strength and strength is vulnerability.

Acknowledging All Selves

Inside each person resides a family of selves, a host of characters that can teach, guide, entertain, and empower us. Some can be vulnerable like the inner child and the lover; others can be fierce like the protector, critic, and rebel. Each has a different way of being in the world. Like our emotions, there are many colors and shades of selves that make up the terrain of our inner landscape. To know and honor them all is a definition of true strength and vulnerability, and part of The "And" Principle's embrace.

Some selves we readily own, are very familiar with, and easily express. Their voices can be loud. Others we are alienated from, repress, and disown. Often their voices can hardly be heard as whispers. One process that I use to get to know, strengthen, and balance all of my selves is Voice Dialogue. It is a powerful technique that gives voice to all of my parts. And whereas this process is about getting to know the selves, it is equally about developing an aware ego that acts like a CEO who integrates them and makes choices in life. It is a skill that you can learn to use on your own, as well as a process that can be facilitated by a psychotherapist or lay counselor. *Voice Dialogue* was created by Drs. Hal and Sidra Stone, and the ideas presented here are from their book *Embracing Ourselves*.[5]

As a brief illustration of a *Voice Dialogue* session facilitated by a psychotherapist, imagine a middle-aged man who is about to travel to another continent alone. The psychotherapist would assist him in giving voice to various selves such as the vulnerable child and the adventurer. Each voice would be asked a series of questions to find out, in part, what it is feeling and what its needs are. Other questions might elicit the self's age, its purpose, and how powerful it is. After both selves have spoken, the client would assume the role of the witness and listen as the psychotherapist repeats back what the voices have said. Then our client would take the role of the aware ego and share what he learned from this process and how he would meet the needs of these two selves as he traveled.

LIKE MOSAICS

We are all like mosaics,
broken pieces,
whole pieces,
all uniquely shaped,
each beautiful,
designed for lessons
to be learned.

Each one
coming together
to form a new whole,
an artistic expression,
a reconfiguration,
a dignified beauty,
forged from sweat and toil,
joy and celebration.

KITTY LOVE

I can kiss your head for hours if I want to.
I can tell you I love you one hundred times a day.
I can smooch and cuddle and talk silly mushy talk to you.
And you won't object.
And you won't get frightened.
And you won't withdraw.

It's so wonderful to not have issues about love.

A TENDER MOMENT

A two-year-old little boy sits on his father's lap on the sidewalk.
They both are looking up at the moon.
The father turns to me and says, "My son loves the moon."
The little boy, arm outstretched to the sky,
excitedly shouts, "Moon! Moon!"

FLIGHT

The largest, most ferocious lion
usually cannot harm the tiny sparrow.

Wouldn't it be wonderful if we all could fly?

SASSY PEOPLE LIVE LONGER

Sassy people live longer.
Being tough, saying it like it is, going for what they want,
and not being so concerned about others.

It's the overly sensitive people who have a hard time.
Being cautious, pleasing everybody, and caring all the time.
It wearies the heart and tires the body.

Sensitive is good.
Unbalanced with sassy, it's dangerous.

Be tough.
Be sensitive.
Be happy.

FIERCE

Fierce life,
sharp tongue,
cutting through false pleasantries.
Knowing that intimacy and truth are brothers.
Sacrificing comfort for love.
Ruled by authenticity,
eased by thoughtfulness.
Demanding congruency.
Listening intently,
discerning what is true and genuine.
Solid ground
to embark on the journey.

MAGIC'S CATALYST

Risk-taking is magic's catalyst.

It sets in motion synchronicity,
and an interconnectedness beyond imagining.

It says to life,
"I will do my part, and be your partner."

It declares,
"I have power, and can affect my world."

It proclaims,
"I am a grand initiator in the universe."

NECTAR

I watched a hummingbird, for what seemed like forever,
foraging flowers, and I said to myself,
"There must be a poem in this."
This little being, chest florescent green,
wings flapping so fast they were a blur,
went from flower to flower
and with such precision inserted its long beak,
destined for nectar.
Its singularity of purpose and inexhaustible energy
impressed me most.
It knows who it is and what it must do,
and when we know the same
nectar also will be our reward.

FULL SPECTRUM

Full spectrum,
all colors,
the power of the sun.

Full spectrum,
wholeness,
realness.
Light and shadow,
boldness and vulnerability,
rising up and falling down.

No missing bricks to weaken the foundation.
No hidden colors ruining the rainbow.

Full spectrum.
Full life.

CHAPTER 5 – QUESTIONS TO PONDER

1. How do you view vulnerability?

   Do you see it in yourself and others as a strength or a weakness?

2. Remember a time when someone close to you was crying. How did you feel?

   Did you try to get them to stop crying or did you assist them in getting their feelings out?

3. In what ways do you express the warrior in yourself?

4. How do you feel when you don't give people what they want? How do you handle others' disapproval?

5. How do you interpret rejection?

   Think of one occasion when you were rejected. Come up with three possible interpretations for the rejection that had nothing to do with you.

6. Reflect upon and acknowledge the specific ways you express strength and vulnerability in your life.

"…*and then the day came when the risk to remain tight in the bud was more painful than the risk it took to blossom.*"

Anais Nin

FREEDOM and DISCIPLINE:

Parenting from The "And" Principle

FREEDOM and DISCIPLINE:

Parenting from The "And" Principle

> *"'The hand that rocks the cradle'*
> *does indeed rock the world."*[6]
> John Bradshaw

I have come to believe that what allows adults to easily live *The "And" Principle* is to have been parented according to it. Parents who live the principle can give this gift to their children, and this is how the world will change. This requires parents to do the work to honor all aspects of themselves. It requires parents to exercise discipline and to foster freedom with their children, realizing that these are interrelated. For it is often discipline that allows for freedom for both parents and children. The discipline of setting limits is what allows children the freedom to explore life without needing to always test limits. The discipline of children delaying gratification has been shown to increase their overall fulfillment as adults. The discipline of listening allows us the freedom to love. The discipline of exercise affords the freedom to enjoy our bodies with agility and strength. Let us all realize that discipline and freedom are merely two sides of the same coin. Now we will look at more of the qualities of an effective parent.

The Ten Qualities of an Effective Parent

1. *Having Emotional Integrity* – Emotional integrity is part of being free. Parents who can feel and appropriately express anger, sadness, love, joy, fear, and excitement can provide a free, safe environment for their children to remain emotionally vibrant. These children will grow up with all their parts intact, having a compass to navigate as adults in their lives.

2. *Providing an Emotionally Satisfying Experience* – Adults and children need loving relationships like they need food and water. Parents who can provide an *emotionally satisfying* experience for their children make it much easier for their children to create fulfilling relationships later in life. *It is very difficult to create as adults what you never experienced as a child.*

3. *Knowing the Self* – Knowing the Self can have enormous consequences on parents' level of fulfillment and on how they raise their children. It can be a great source of *guidance* in the process of parenting and can take the form of consulting and following their intuition. When children see that spiritual essence shining through their parents' eyes, they feel recognized, comforted, and loved. From this place, it is easier for a parent to say, "I love you not because of anything that you will ever do in this life. I love

you just because of who you are." Such unconditional love creates the freedom for children to be themselves.

4. *Feeling Good and Feeling Good About Yourself* – Children tend to feel good about themselves when they are around parents who feel good about themselves. They get a sense that they are OK and that life is OK. *From this secure feeling, they can get on with the business of growing up.* When parents are unhappy most of the time, children often personalize the experience and think that they did something wrong or that they are somehow not enough. Parents need not feel good all the time; however, feeling good much of the time will improve the quality of the parenting.

5. *Being Loving and Physically Nurturing* – Emotionally healthy parents love and physically nurture their children in appropriate ways. The importance of being able to sink into the warm embrace of a parent cannot be overestimated. Touch often lets children know that they are not alone.

6. *Fostering Authenticity* – Parents who are reasonably whole inside do not use children to fulfill missing pieces of their lives. From this fulfillment they foster, and don't hinder, their child's authentic expression. Being authentic is freedom. Children naturally love their parents. If their parents are usually unhappy in work and in their marriage, many children lose themselves in their often unconscious desire to fulfill their parents' needs. Happy parents do not need that much from their children and therefore can more easily foster their children's uniqueness. Being basically satisfied in their marriage, they do not need their children to become surrogate spouses and take care of them. Being basically fulfilled in their work, their children do not need

to become "the doctor that they never became." Part of fostering authenticity and freedom is to allow children to separate when the time is appropriate, not being too dependent on them.

7. *Understanding Child Development* – To be effective, parents must understand the developmental stages and tasks of their children and be able to fulfill the needs of each stage. This understanding informs parents of their children's physical, cognitive, emotional, and spiritual abilities and allows parents to have realistic expectations of them. This is part of a disciplined approach to parenting.

8. *Setting Limits and Teaching Discipline* – Effective parents set appropriate limits and risk their children's displeasure. Children need solid boundaries to bounce up against as they grow and change. Otherwise they will always be testing limits, and cannot easily get on with learning their next developmental task. Related to setting limits is teaching children the discipline of how to solve problems and have strong boundaries.

9. *Focusing on the Positive* – Effective parents notice, validate, and mirror back their children's positive attributes and behaviors. Studies have shown that most children get approximately 250 "no"s to 40 "yes"es a day. This negative orientation weakens their self-esteem. The idea is to suggest to children *what to do* more often than what not to do. As a pre-school teacher, this orientation saved me. During clean-up time for example, my approach was to notice all the students that were cleaning up well and give them loud verbal recognition. Soon all the kids wanted to be recognized and followed suit. If teachers only focused on

negative behavior and criticized the children who were not cleaning up, they would die from exhaustion!

10. *Being a Good Communicator* – Communication is part of what holds a relationship together. Parents need to know effective communication skills and teach them to their children. This is part of teaching discipline. All relationships involve conflict at some point and without effective communication, intimacy is lost. Parents need to be able to demonstrate to their children that conflict can be resolved and intimacy restored.

A Note to Non-Parents

If you don't have your own children, you can apply this chapter to yourself by thinking of ways that you do parent your friends, their children, and your pets. And we all have an inner child inside ourselves. So you can apply these ten qualities to that inner relationship. It is my sincere hope that you will find this chapter relevant to that inner relationship.

Nature and Nurture

For children to thrive in life, it is very helpful for them to have loving parents who possess the previously mentioned qualities (nurture) and to be born with a good biochemistry (nature). I know a handful of people who have both, and their lives have been blessed. Some children didn't get either. These are children who didn't have one really good connection in their early lives. Their parents did not possess enough of the qualities of effective parents, and as a result they sustained emotional injuries. In addition to these injuries and lack of nurturance, they inherited poor biochemistry. This means, for example, that they don't have enough neurotransmitters in their brains and are prone to depression, or they have too much adrenalin in their systems and are prone to have anxiety issues. *This double loss sets them up to struggle in life.* Simplistic notions that life is good and abundant, you can easily create what you want, or happiness is a choice, don't seem very helpful to these people. This does not mean they are destined to suffer forever or that they can't create the life they want. It just means that they will have significant challenges that need to be understood and treated *realistically.* Psychotherapy and medication may be necessary. Compensating for this double loss by having a life coach or mentor and being in a support group can be effective. (I am a great proponent of compensation.) I do not hear the voices of these people in the world of literature or song, and *someone needs to speak for them.* So I am speaking for them now in this reflection and in the poetry that follows.

Once children are emotionally injured, and later as adults develop issues and challenges in their lives, I think it is helpful for them to have reasonable expectations about these issues being *healed.* From my personal and professional experience, I have come to the conclusion that these issues are often more *managed* than healed. And I feel that healing takes place to different degrees. For example, a child raised by depressed parents who often felt hopeless might as an adult find himself naturally pessimistic. This deeply ingrained pessimism might not change dramatically or be *completely* healed, yet he can learn to manage it. This management could take the form of many of the skills presented in this book including: 1) learning to assess the rationality of his pessimistic thoughts and then replacing irrational thoughts with rational ones; and 2) using various *Voice Dialogue* techniques to help him balance his pessimistic self through building up the strength of his optimistic self.

An Ounce of Prevention
Is Worth a Pound of Cure

The relationship between parent and child has unparalleled potential for intimacy. It also has unparalleled potential for emotional injury and alienation. This potentiality is due to many things. A child is part of your blood, comes from your body, and is utterly vulnerable in your care. It is said we are a "we" before we become an "I".[7] A child swims in the fluid of its mother's womb. It is as close to mother as is humanly possible. It feels everything she feels. Held in a father's arms, a newborn is without boundaries and is one with his embrace. What an opportunity! What a responsibility! These early impressions will have a powerful effect on the destiny of your child. So prepare your field carefully. Plant your seeds with love. Cultivate and water well and remember that young plants need extra sensitivity and protection.

Some children are fortunate to grow up in a nurturing fertile field. For them, I delight. Their futures look hopeful. For others, their fields are dry and parched and full of strangling weeds. For these children, my heart aches. And that is why I have dedicated most of my career to helping children grow up in a healthy way. I have been practicing psychotherapy for over twenty years, and I see that many people spend much of their adult lives trying to change the habits and patterns created by early emotional injury and trauma. Prevention, a lessening of the damage in the first place, is an investment that will bring great dividends. *My vision is that people will wait to have children until after they have cultivated the self-esteem that will allow them to demonstrate the qualities of an effective parent.*

Parenting from *The "And" Principle* is an *exciting adventure* in creating a new kind of child and family. From this principle, the true potential of family life is more easily realized. Children raised in this way will more easily grow up knowing who they are, what they feel, and what they want. Their authenticity will flourish and will not need extensive therapy to emerge. *I invite you all to join me in this grand experiment!* It will produce a new generation of children who will start off where many of us only get to late in our lives, if at all. Parenting from *The "And" Principle* will change this world for the better.

FREEDOM AND DISCIPLINE105

YOUR FULFILLMENT

Your fulfillment
creates a space
which fosters the growth
of your child's authentic self.

Unfettered by your needs, aspirations, and dreams,
this space encourages the discovery and fulfillment
of your child's own aspirations and dreams.

Your fulfillment
helps bestow on your children
the gift of themselves,
for which they will grow up
and love you.

SHRIEKING WITH JOY

A little boy,
shrieking with joy,
walks across the grass
into his mother's loving arms.

Life doesn't get better than that.

A BABY'S FOOTPRINTS

A baby's footprints in the sand.
Cute little impressions.
So full of promise!
I follow them up the beach.
Where are they leading, I wonder?
I hope to blue skies and billowing white clouds.

PURRS

A father braids his daughter's hair
while she marches in place.
They are waiting in a restaurant line.
So warm, so close.
She looks up at him and smiles.
His heart purrs.

ON PARENTING

If your children are objects
to fulfill your needs,

chances are they will give up their dance
to dance with you,

and they may spend much of their lives
just trying to figure out who they are.

LOST

Not honoring a child's feelings
is like robbing a bear cub of its instincts.
It's lost in the forest,
lost in the world.

TWO IMPRINTS

A new fresh life,
utterly vulnerable,
awaits your imprint
and the imprint of your mate.

Before conceiving a child
ask yourself,
"Will these two imprints
be able to live peacefully
inside this child?"

I WONDER

I look into the face of a homeless man and I wonder,
"What authentic, powerful being lurks behind
those drunken eyes and ruddy skin?"
"What would he have become with proper love and care?"

I'd love to see that beautiful sculpture emerge,
as I chip away at the adaptive stone
that covers his strength and beauty.
"Will it ever emerge?" I ask myself.
"Or will it remain forever hidden
from a world that needed his gift?"

INSIDIOUS

It is insidious how we attract what we've known,
how we create relationships like those from childhood.
Beautiful, sensitive, giving people, with a weak link.
A link that connects them to their past, sabotaging their lives.
An unresponsive father,
a narcissistic mother,
creating patterns that yearn to repeat themselves.
A repetition compulsion, unconscious, insidious.
A hidden script that creates a drama filled with tragedy.
Tend to the wound.
Rewrite the play.
It is time for a romantic novel with a happy ending.

SHORTEN THE FUSE

Little precious ones with *noble* needs.
Needs as natural as the trees and the sun.
Needs often unfulfilled.
Not seen.
Not heard.
Attunement lacking.
An attunement that would have led them
directly to themselves,
the salvation of their lives.
Like skewed lines never meeting,
their parents often missed the mark.
Thousands of interactions
where they were *emotionally unfulfilled*.
Each mishap *lengthening the fuse*,
lengthening their tolerance for discord and frustration.
Children now grown,
they tolerate so much pain.
Their fuse is so long.
Skewed lines seem normal to them.
Children fulfilled
would give *five minutes*
to what they devote *five years*,
or a *lifetime*.
Oh precious ones,
you deserve *the best* that life has to offer.
Raise the bar.
Shorten the fuse.
Shorten the fuse.
Shorten the fuse!

AFTER ALL WE GIVE

After all we give
day after day
and year after year,
if we are happy enough
to let our children be different from us
and separate from us,
if we can accept our children's feelings
whether they be happy, sad, angry, or afraid,
if we can foster their uniqueness
and encourage them to lead their own lives,
then we will have a good chance
that they will grow up
and like us.

UNIQUENESS

You are here
to witness and nurture
your children's unfolding
and to cherish
that which is only in them.

WITH ANTICIPATION

Watch your children grow
as if you were watching seeds unfold,
the types of which you knew not,
and with anticipation
look on as they reveal their beauty.

ODE TO A BABY OAK

Hi, little one.
You are so beautiful!
Being a great admirer of your older brothers and sisters,
I know what you will become.
Your trunk is now thin and moves with the wind,
yet someday your trunk will be so thick no wind will make
    it sway.
Your branches are narrow and can carry little weight,
yet someday birds will nest in your branches,
and rest on them singing into the night.
Your trunk is now smooth like a child's face,
yet someday it will be craggy and textured
by time passed and experience gained.
Your branches meander now with slight twists and turns,
yet someday they will streak like veins of lightning across
    the sky.
I know the glory you will become.
It is inevitable as long as your needs are met,
and your needs are simple and few.
Sun, water, and respect.
Needs met, potentiality realized.
Needs met, the fruition of your design.
Needs met, the fulfillment of the dream that you are now
    in miniature.
Oh, what will you experience? I do not know.
I do know you've chosen a beautiful place to grow up in,
surrounded by elders and mountains covered with green velvet.
Blessings, little oak.
I wish for you long life, good life.

CHAPTER 6 – QUESTIONS TO PONDER

1. What were two qualities that you most admired in each of your parents as you were growing up?

   How have these qualities affected you in your adult life?

2. (If you are a parent) If there was only one gift you could give your child, what would it be?

   Why did you choose that particular gift?

3. List two ways you were parented that were destructive.

   (If you are a parent) What could you do that would insure that you don't make the same mistake with your children (i.e., if your mother denied your emotions, you could get in therapy and develop emotional integrity that would enable you to accept and celebrate your children's emotions)?

4. Reflect on an area of your life where discipline brought with it the gift of freedom (i.e., the discipline of setting boundaries brought you the freedom to get what you wanted).

5. Did your early childhood experiences sensitize you to certain issues, setting you up to seek a certain life path or career?

   If so, how?

6. (If you are not a parent) How could you apply the ten qualities of an effective parent to the way you relate to your inner child?

7. What do you think are the three most important qualities for a parent to have, and why?

*"It is the child's feeling about being
loved or unloved that affects
how he will develop."*
Dorothy Corkille Briggs

7

MOVEMENT
and
STILLNESS

Reflection on

MOVEMENT and STILLNESS

If the gift of stillness is clarity of purpose,
the gift of movement is the manifestation of desire.
Bill E. Goldberg

Balance is one of the most important words in the English language. It is great to spend time alone, yet too much solitude can be disturbing. Chocolate is delicious, yet overindulging will make you sick. Pleasing others is wonderful, yet done to excess you lose yourself. Certainly, leading a balanced life is the royal road to fulfillment.

To seek to balance movement and stillness is a worthy goal. Yet it is rarely attained, due to the changes and demands of daily living. The closer we get to it, the more satisfied we are. Nature demonstrates balance as it places trees beside rivers, for trees are master teachers of stillness and rivers are of movement.

The gifts of stillness are immeasurable. Stillness allows for contact with the divine. A still mind gives us a glimpse of another reality beyond time and space. Stillness can open the heart just as moving too fast can close it. It lets us access our feelings and is a gateway to intimacy. It is in the stillness of the moment that lovers embrace. Stillness connects us to our intuition and to inner guidance. It is also an essential element of health, as the body needs rest to restore itself.

In my life, meditation has been a long-standing practice to cultivate stillness. I have often thought that meditation is life itself, for it allows me actually to experience *life* as opposed to *my mind about life*. And there is a big difference between the two. Thinking about a sunset is very different than, with a still mind, experiencing it. One is ho-hum, the other takes my breath away.

Movement is as essential to life as is stillness. As I mentioned earlier, "keeping it all moving" is my core philosophy. I believe that it is the paradigm of health. And whether it is through communicating, risk-taking, exercising, or creating a painting, life longs for movement and self-expression. A main way I keep things moving is through dance. For the past twenty-five years, I have been privileged to have movement and dance in my life. On most days, I focus in on the sensations of my body, put on some music, and let my body lead. My body has led me to a more intimate relationship with myself and the people in my world.

Movement and action are also central to having an effective, productive life. There is a story about a man stranded out at sea in a small boat. For hours he prayed for help, content just to pray. Then inwardly he heard the admonition, "Pray, *and row to shore!*" Like this man, many people err on the side of prayer, affirmation, and visualization without the commensurate balance of creating an action plan and taking responsibility for their lives. No business would run this way, yet many people practice magical thinking and allow initiative to remain on the sidelines.

Creativity and productivity depend, in part, on being proactive. The word "satisfaction" means enough action.

One of the most powerful tools to get myself moving, acting, and taking risks is to make an agreement with another person. To set up action steps, deadlines, and consequences with someone else creates the support and accountability I sometimes need to overcome inertia and procrastination. *One of the most important questions you can ask yourself is: "What will I be able to do alone, and what will I need help with?"*

Gabrielle Roth, the creator of *The Five Rhythms*, an ecstatic dance practice, tells us, "The fastest way I've found to still the mind and be aware of the moment is to move the body."[8] Of the rhythms she teaches, the last is stillness. So in reality, movement and stillness are interwoven like threads of the same cloth. Let us embrace both as the powerful cycles of nature that they are. For stillness without movement is incomplete and ineffective, and movement without stillness is often misguided and exhausting. The journey towards the balance is the adventure of life.

TRUTH

Truth is so simple.
It walks with a hush.
Its voice is soft-spoken.
It could easily be missed
if you move too fast.
It is freely found in the wilderness,
where things move slowly,
when you attune to the pace
that the trees grow.

HOLDING VIGIL

A grove of oak trees holds vigil
like the elders of a church
for the congregation.

These wise ones came here to stand still,
while the earth turns,
and its inhabitants run frantically
searching for many things.

THE INFINITE

The stillness of pond reflects beauty
like a quiet mind reveals the infinite.

FOLLOW THE LEAD

Intuition
Guidance
Hunches
Ways out of the darkness.

CIRCLE OF REMEMBERING

Sitting quietly in meditation,
I join the community of others,
who each day
traverse inner landscape
to venture into the mystery of themselves,
and experience the vision
that comes from a still mind.

This pilgrimage connects us
in a circle of remembering.

KEEP IT ALL MOVING

Breathe
Move
Feel
Dance
Communicate
Forgive
Create
Risk
Meditate
Serve.

Blocked rivers
become stagnant.
Blocked bodies
become sick.

Health is fluidity
and self-expression.

WILD MAN

Dancing fool
Crazed by the beat
Out of my mind
And into my feet.

SWEAT

At first self-conscious,
I dance until
my sweat creates
a river
that takes me to
my soul.
Eyes closed,
I disappear
into the waves,
and all that's left
is rhythm.
Laughter ripples through my body.
Joy arises
past walls that were there
just moments before.
Moving until
my sweat erodes
those walls
that surround my heart.
Beyond those walls
is life,
real life.

WHY CONTAIN THE DANCE
TO THE DANCE FLOOR

Why contain the dance to the dance floor
when ocean sands and peaceful meadows
provide such willing stages.
And the dance is so natural and free,
and feels so good surrounded by the Mother,
the most accepting audience.
Let the rustling of leaves be your music
and the warm sun your inspiration
as you dance for the spirit that gives you life,
moves your limbs, and whispers gently in your ear,
as the wind.

OUT OF THE COMFORT ZONE

Out of the comfort zone
is the incubator of dreams.

It's that uneasy anxiousness,
butterflies in your gut,
and pounding heart
that is the alchemy of hope,
the watering of seeds,
and the prelude to the harvesting of fruit.

Leave the comfort of inertia
and the languid pools of thought
not ripening into action,
and move into turbulence.
A turbulence that rearranges rocks
and creates a new landscape
chiseled by storm.

It is here that creations emerge
that will delight your spirit
and move your heart into contentment.

A SMALL OPENING

An immense melting glacier
sits atop a mountain of stone.
It finds a small opening
and that is all it needs
to enter inside.

It cascades down with a powerful force
careening against cavernous walls
forming a magnificent river below.

An entire river comes through a small opening.

And so in life,
taking a risk
can create a small opening,
that releases a possibility
to enter a whole new world.

A whole new world can come through a small opening.

CHAPTER 7 – QUESTIONS TO PONDER

1. Reflect on several occasions when you felt deep stillness. Where were you? What made these experiences possible?

2. How much stillness do you need in your relationships (i.e., eating quietly or relaxing at home)?

3. Regarding movement and stillness, which is the predominant rhythm in you?

4. Describe three gifts that stillness brings to your life.

5. Describe three gifts that movement offers.

6. When you have difficulty motivating yourself to get something done, what helps you get into motion (i.e., getting someone to do the activity with you, visualizing the end result, or making a commitment to another person that you will complete a certain task)?

7. In what ways do you take responsibility for your life? In what ways do you not?

8. Reflect upon and acknowledge two of your most triumphant life experiences that resulted principally from your own initiative.

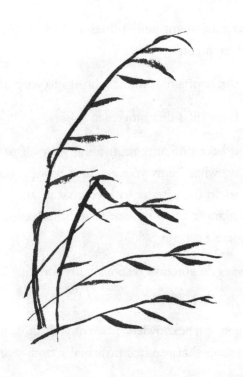

THE WIND
and
THE REED:

Celebrating
the Creative Process

Reflection on

THE WIND and THE REED:

Celebrating
the Creative Process

"Creation is still going on...
the creative forces are as great
and as active today as they have ever been...
tomorrow's morning will be as heroic as any of the world."
Henry Beston

One of our most noble qualities as a species is our ability to create. As we create, we align ourselves with the natural world which is an ultimate statement of creativity. And then we find ourselves, like nature, creating in so many beautiful ways. Recall the majesty and elegance of a dance performance, or the music of your favorite recording artist or group and the joy they have given you. Recall the pleasure of a well-prepared meal, the delight of seeing beautiful architecture, or the feeling in your heart when you are moved by a poetic voice that lets you know you aren't alone.

The creative process is mysterious and many have been intrigued by what inspires it. I would like to explore several possibilities. Firstly, creativity comes from the Self, which is a source of immense creative potential. Creativity enters the domain of the spiritual as the artist taps into an inner wellspring of inspiration. A principal role of the artist is to prepare a path for the enunciation, to still and purify the mind enough for a deeper current to emerge. The artist first becomes receptive enough to *hear*, and then he or she writes, composes, paints, dances. The artist is also the audience in a way, observing the creative impulse as it reveals itself. A wondrous experience for the spiritually adventurous!

A second source of creative expression is the artist's angst, joy, love, fear, and conflict. This is the aspect of art that is as personal as the Self is impersonal. This is the song of grief about your father abandoning you. This is the song of triumph as you fall in love. This is the painting of a landscape that takes your breath away. Here the artist is at times extremely vulnerable, willing to expose parts of him or herself that many would rather keep close to the chest and seen by the few and the trusted. I appreciate those who disclose the raw impulses of their lives for the benefit of the many. I also respect the boundaries of those who are more private, for we all have our place in this world.

It is also said that the creative process comes from holding the tension of opposites, and I believe this is true. I see it in the desire for growth and the need for security, the draw towards love and the fear of loss, the rise of self-confidence and the contraction of self-doubt. How do we reconcile this complex world of polarities? The navigation of this territory begins with awareness of the opposites. It proceeds with their acceptance, and it often results in creative expression in order to find resolution. The artist's path is to find this resolution through a new way of seeing, expressing, or acting in the world.

Artistic expression expands us, inspires us, and connects us. As I have gotten more involved in the artistic world and the creative life, I have become fascinated by the experience of "creative intimacy." This term is best described through examples. A cynical middle-aged man watches a romantic play and feels inspired to open to love again. New parents read a poem about how to raise a healthy child and both start to weep. A young woman viewing religious art at a museum feels spirit's presence. These are cherished moments. The synapse has been bridged. The artist's experience so *resonates* with the audience that it evokes a pure, deep, visceral response. This is the wonder of creative intimacy. And it does not matter if the artist is living or deceased, residing next door or on another continent, for the creative spirit is alive and has the power to traverse time and space through the language of the heart.

I can't leave the topic of creativity without mentioning the metaphor of childbirth. For writing a book, choreographing a dance, or constructing a building are births in their own right with all the attendant challenges, successes, chaos, and mess. Then there is the privilege, joy, exhilaration, and pride that creativity, in its many forms, offers those who wish to partake. Like childbirth, some projects come with short, easy labors, while others are excruciating and long. For me, the process of writing encompasses myriad feelings, some enjoyable and some not. Yet overall, I find the process to be one of the greatest pleasures of my life. I have the desire to give birth to my creative best and share it with others. And in the giving, I hope to join those courageous souls who have done the same, enriching and blessing the lives of so many.

An Empowering Applause

One of my intentions in writing this chapter is to inspire and support you to engage your creativity more fully. In the spirit of this support, I will end this reflection with a vision I had called *"An Empowering Applause."* A poet had just given an inspiring reading. The crowd was overjoyed and gave the writer a wonderful applause. The poet graciously received the recognition and then said, "Thank you so much. It was a pleasure to read for you. Now I would like all of us to give a standing ovation for the one spirit who comes through everyone in many different ways." In this vision, everyone then stands up and the applause is much stronger than it was for the poet alone. The audience leaves the hall with dignity, each feeling their own power and strength. They hold their heads a little higher, and their focus is not so much on the poet's talent but on the greatness of the spirit that flows through us all.

CULTIVATING RECEPTIVITY

Cultivating receptivity,
the pathway to creativity.
An invitation for spirit to enter.
Passive, open, allowing,
patient, yin.

Joyously anticipating inspiration.

A humble partner
with an open, outstretched hand,
eagerly engaging synergy.

WILLINGNESS

Sometimes
a willingness
is all that's asked for.
Just to open the door,
and like a passing stream
with a rhythm and song of its own,
spirit rushes through
demanding immediate listening
or it's gone in an instant.

THE CREATIVE PROCESS

Holding the tension of opposites,
embracing paradox,
and transcending the mind that creates duality
go to the heart of the creative process.

FLOWERING

The alchemy of pain
is the flowering of dreams.

MANIFESTATION

We have many selves, many voices.
When they all are in alignment,
when they all agree on a particular goal,
we more easily manifest it.

A LIVING SPRING

My poetry is a living spring.
It refreshes, informs, and enlightens.
It is an answer to my questions,
wise counsel, and a beloved friend.
Expressing with a graceful spontaneity,
it is a way spirit shows me it is very near,
a companion walking closely.

THE WIND AND THE REED

The wind and the reed,
the Power and the personality,
both in need of each other.
Without the reed,
the wind makes little sound.
Without people,
the Power has limited reach.
Partnership is the name
of the game.
An adventure of co-creation.
Each player important,
honored, sacred.
The wind and the reed,
the Power and the personality,
both in need of each other.

(The Power refers to the Self.
The personality refers to humanity.)

THE ALCHEMIST

Life is alchemy,
one thing becomes another.

The seed becomes the tree,
the flower, the fruit.
Coal becomes a diamond,
sand, a pearl.

The river becomes the cloud,
the cloud, rain,
rain, the river.

The earth changes into food,
and sunlight becomes all living things.

We transform our experiences also.
Our pain becomes compassion,
our suffering, art,
our problems teach us life's lessons.

Becoming the alchemist
is part of our healing,
using every experience
for our movement towards wholeness.

Alchemy,
what a beautiful word.
It goes to the heart of creation.

THE SKY SPEAKS

A massive explosion,
the sky speaks.
Commotion, chaos, collision.
An uproarious sound
and then rain,
mud, moisture, mischief.

The world is a glorious, messy place.

A PANOPLY OF COLOR

A panoply of color,
an alchemical rainbow.
The earth has become flowers.
Exquisite scented roses.
Yellow petals tinged with pink.
Deep royal reds
expressing love's heart pulsing passion.
An unfolding swirling design
that like a spiral galaxy
beckons us into its core.
An inevitable flowering,
a celebration of life's wonder and beauty.

CHAPTER 8 – QUESTIONS TO PONDER

1. Pretend that before you were born you knew your life's mission, and were given certain talents so that you could complete it.

   What would those talents be?

2. What can you do/create that no one else can?

   How can you make yourself indispensable by expressing your uniqueness?

3. Which creative acts bring pleasure to your body?

   What comes naturally to you that is easy for you (i.e., dancing, cooking, public speaking, or writing)?

4. How do you conceptualize creativity?

   Where do you think creative inspiration comes from?

5. Which creative artists do you admire, and why?

"Those who contemplate the beauty of the earth find reserves of strength that will endure as long as life lasts."

Rachel Carson

ONENESS
and
SEPARATENESS

ONENESS and SEPARATENESS

"And we come trailing starlight,
whether we know it or not."[9]

Roger Housden

L ife is mysterious. And from a young age, I felt the mystery as I looked out at the stars and felt the wide expanse of space. The context of life, being on a tiny ball whirling amongst galaxies, preoccupied me in my younger years. As I have grown older, I have come to appreciate and feel comfortable living with the mystery, enjoying the questions that are raised by life.

Oneness and separateness shows us the mysterious nature of life. It is challenging to write about because the experience of oneness comes when we transcend the mind, yet the mind and language are what we use to describe it. The subject is really beyond words. That said, I will offer one response to the mystery for your consideration.

We live in a multi-dimensional universe where different levels of reality occur simultaneously. There is the relative world of duality: the play of subject and object in time and space. This is the world of separateness in which we experience ourselves as individuals living our lives with our daily responsibilities. Then there is absolute reality: the experience of oneness beyond time and space in which subject and object merge like streams that have become the ocean. Both realities must be dealt with for oneness is real, *and* checkbooks must be balanced and bills paid that are in your individual name. An ultimate goal of *The "And" Principle* is to experience relative reality from the context of the absolute, to have experiences arise and subside and to constantly merge back into our source. To keep coming back to the ground of our being. This is *an integrated enlightenment.*

Many of us live much of the time in duality, our lives being defined by our personalities, sex, age, and culture. We have families or live alone, do our jobs, and work to fulfill endless daily tasks. The world of separateness has many great joys as well as many frustrations and difficulties. And as wonderful and challenging as individual existence can be, the world of separation is ultimately limited. For many of us, there comes a time when we need and sense that there is more. When fame and fortune, good deeds and great accomplishments, still leave us yearning. We want the infinite. The experience of oneness is what satisfies this longing. Most people have had glimpses of it. In nature, making love, or playing music many people have temporarily felt the euphoria that comes from getting lost in something bigger. It is from the thirst for this experience of oneness that many pursue a spiritual path.

I turned to meditation, being in nature, and ecstatic dance. With meditation, I was fortunate to meet and study with a teacher who assisted me in awakening to a new level of spiritual energy and an experience of the Self, which furthered the blossoming of my spiritual life. As my meditation practice deepened, so did a sense of oneness.

Nature has also been a place where I experience this spiritual energy. The wilderness continues to be a major source of wisdom, guidance, and nourishment in my life. It provides access to the Self, a vibrant, spiritual presence. One of the beautiful things about being alive is that there are so many ways that lead to this presence.

The dance floor has been another place where I have received inspiration and felt intimacy and oneness. Great music opens my heart, and the dance consistently reveals my spirit. I love to merge with the music and get lost in the beat.

It is this dipping into oneness that fuels my day. It is the attunement with spirit that brings grace into my life. Otherwise, I bump into things. I'm just not in synch and my day does not flow well. Do you know the feeling? Meditation, being in nature, and ecstatic dance are practical experiences for me, on one level. They create a more enjoyable, relaxed, healthy, and effective life.

In conclusion, enjoy the dance of oneness and separateness: two dimensions, two loves, two worlds, our worlds — be with it all.

PART OF SOMETHING BIGGER

People love becoming part of something bigger.

A couple strolling down a deserted beach
disappearing into the expanse of sea and sky.

A man hiking along a twisting trail
dwarfed by the mountains surrounding him.

A congregation immersed in song
carried into the rapture of spirit.

Lovers enthralled in passion
transcending into waves of bliss.

We love losing ourselves.
We love being carried away by something bigger,
something mightier than our little selves and little minds.

Little selves, little minds
connecting with something bigger,
our salvation.

A GLORIOUS DESIGN

Circles cascading out
on a river's pooling water.
Ripples of destiny.
Venturing out from their centers,
intersecting with each other
like people in an emerging tapestry
of connectedness.
Such a glorious design,
two circles intersecting.
Part of the stream of life,
meeting in a place of immeasurable beauty,
and then moving on together
towards an ocean of immense power,
varied moods, and oneness.

A LOOSENING

Bare feet on warm sand,
a tight spring loosens.
Soft soil,
an open portal
that receives all.
The call of roots,
origins,
simplicity.
I lie down,
arms outstretched,
and sacrifice my smallness
to Father Sky.

HUMANITY

We all see the same moon at night, the same stars.
We all feel pain when we lose someone dear.
We all feel afraid when we enter the unknown.
We all long for love.
We all feel joy that lifts us to the heavens,
and we all create, and dance, and sing.

We come in many colors, shapes, and forms.
I've traveled the world and seen.
We come in all shades of brown, black, yellow, red, and white.
Some with large bodies, some small.
Some with straight hair, some curly.
Eyes of all types and sizes.
Yet underneath this *thin packaging* we are so much the same.
See the heart inside those eyes that longs for warmth
    and acceptance,
and let's love one another.

THE CIRCLE OF LIFE

This beautiful room
is surrounded by the sounds of critters.
A symphony of little ones
reminding me of the circle of life.
A circle of chirps and rustling in the leaves,
of fluttering wings and acorns falling on rooftops.
A circle of wondrous expression.
Each critter with its own little way in this big world.
One speaks and the other responds.
Nature's conversation.
And behind it all, there is a hum.
I think it's bees.
Creating a mantra,
a backdrop for the songs of birds.

DRINKING A CLOUD

I'm thirsty
and have no water,
so I start eating an apple
and realize
I'm drinking a cloud.

ANDROMEDA

Last night I saw Andromeda
appearing as a ball of diffuse light
in the far, far distance.
My first vision of other galaxies.
Contemplating other worlds,
my perspective changed forever.

MYSTICS

Mystics contain all religions,
paths, faiths, and scriptures.

They see the One in the many
and the many in the One.

SERVICE

We've gone as far as we can go being concerned
    with ourselves.
At some point our growth is dependent on giving.
Our personal striving can eventually run us into a wall,
for self-concern is finite
and our soul yearns for the infinite.
Serving others offers a key to the kingdom
and opens the door to boundless awareness.

CHAPTER 9 – QUESTIONS TO PONDER

1. What is your response to the mystery of life?

2. What is your philosophy of life?

   Why do you think you are here?

   What brings meaning to your existence?

3. List four of your life's core values.

4. What do you turn to when things get tough?

5. In what ways are you grounded and practical?

   Do you have savings for a rainy day?

6. How would you answer the question, "Who am I?"

   How do you identify yourself?

7. What brings you an experience of oneness? of awe?

8. Think of a time when you experienced a feeling of oneness.

   How did you feel?

   How did this experience affect you?

Epilogue:
The Gift of Continuums

The concept of "continuums" has allowed me to more fully live *The "And" Principle*. Continuums put a finishing touch on *"And"* by letting all the dualities and polarities soften. Let me explain.

The mind tends to think in terms of categories. It likes to quantify, label, and define. These are ways it organizes itself, creates goals, and makes sense of the world. Categories are an essential part of personal effectiveness and an important part of this book. Yet, like everything else, they are limited. "Married," "a parent," "successful," "unsuccessful," "happy," or "sad" are examples of personal labels and categorical thinking. This type of thinking tends to be black or white, all or nothing. I am either "married" or I'm not. I am either "a parent" or I'm not. Yet taking a deeper view, these ideas can be half-truths. *The balancing point for categorical thinking is the salve of continuums.*

Continuums see life not as black or white but as a spectrum of vibrant colors. It sees *qualities* and not just labels. Being "married" therefore is seen as possessing the quality or ability to be emotionally intimate. From the perspective of continuums, an unmarried couple that is truly intimate, would be more "married" than a married couple that lacks closeness. For you can be married and not united, and you can live in the same house and be worlds apart. Being "a parent," from the perspective of continuums, would be a wide-open field and would include parenting yourself, holding a friend while she cries, lovingly brushing your cat, or tending your garden.

All-or-nothing categorical thinking can also impede taking action. You might think, "I must clean the whole kitchen." "I need to walk for one hour." Continuums says, "I will wash one dish." "I will walk for five minutes." Continuums get you started, and starting is often a key to creating momentum.

For me, the concept of continuums offers a special gift by giving me back all of my experiences. Its inclusive nature encompasses so much of how I feel, who I am, and what I have accomplished. It acknowledges all the ways that love and success are already in my life. It lets me know that my life is happening now and that my goals are in process. Through this, it assists me in being more satisfied in the present. The mind will often try to convince me that fulfillment will always be happening in the future. Yet life is mainly the journey. It is about learning and growing. If you are waiting for the category of "arrival" or "destination," you may spend most of your life in desire and longing. Desire and longing are fine as long as they are balanced by contentment and peace. The mind can also tend towards grandiosity and rob you of small things. Yet all things begin small. Each flower begins as a bud. So remember to celebrate modest gestures, for it is small steps that keep things moving. And whether these steps lead to a big accomplishment or not, it isn't so important if you enjoy the ride. Continuums help you enjoy the ride.

To further illustrate the difference between categorical thinking and thinking in terms of continuums, I will present various examples. When reading the examples in the right column, know that thinking in terms of continuums would include the examples under categorical thinking *and* would also be open to other options.

Thinking in Terms of Categories	*Thinking in Terms of Continuums*
Going on a vacation to Yosemite.	Visiting a local park or nearby beach, or visualizing being in a forest.
Being in love only means having a romantic relationship in your life.	Being in love can take the form of romantic love, friendship, love of spirit, or being dedicated to serve in some way.
I live only at my primary residence.	I live in many places. All the locations I visit or vacation at are also my homes, and places to which I will return.
Wealth is only making over $250,000 a year.	Wealth is also making $40,000 a year, being capable of living in the present moment, and having love in your life.
Publishing a poetry book.	Reading ten poems and distributing them to friends.
Eating a five-course meal.	Enjoying a nutritious, well-balanced snack to hold you over.
I have one self, and it is gentle and kind.	I have many selves: some gentle and kind, some angry and rough.
Having a one-hour conversation with a friend to share all the details of your day.	Talking with a friend for five minutes, sharing highlights of the day.

EPILOGUE – QUESTIONS TO PONDER

1. Do you tend to think more in terms of continuums or categories?

   List two benefits of each type of thinking.

2. Consider three labels you use to describe yourself.

   How are these labels limiting or half-truths?

3. Contemplate two areas of your life in which you have a difficult time getting moving.

   Applying the concept of continuums, what small step could you take to get started?

4. List three things that you would like to accomplish.

   How have these things, to some degree, already manifested in your life?

Footnotes and Further Explorations: Gold from the Riverbed

CHAPTER 2

1. Burns, David, M.D., *Feeling Good, The New Mood Therapy.* New York: Avon Books, 1980

   This book includes a list of cognitive distortions that is powerful, insightful, and invaluable.

2. Moore, Thomas, *Original Self.* New York: HarperCollins, 2000

   The *Original Self* is about living with authenticity, passion, and originality.

CHAPTER 3

3. Naomi Shihab Nye, "Kindness," *Words Under the Words: Selected Poems by Naomi Shihab Nye,* Portland, Oregon: Far Corner Books, 1995

   A wonderful collection of poems by a poet whom I deeply appreciate.

CHAPTER 4

4. Goldberg, Bill E., *Protecting the Diamond, Communication Skills to Create and Maintain Intimacy in Your Life.* Los Angeles: Self-Published, 1997

   This CD presents a dynamic communication system that includes practical and effective tools for protecting the love in your relationships.

CHAPTER 5

5. Stone, Hal and Sidra, *Embracing Ourselves, The Voice Dialogue Manual.* Mill Valley: Nataraj Publishing, 1989

Voice Dialogue is an authoritative exploration of the psychology of selves.

CHAPTER 6

6-7. Bradshaw, John, *Homecoming.* New York: Bantam Books, 1990

This powerful workbook can assist you in reclaiming your inner child.

CHAPTER 7

8. Roth, Gabrielle, *Maps to Ecstasy.* Novato: New World Library, 1998

The maps that Gabrielle Roth presents, which include *The Five Rhythms*, can be life-changing. Her other books include *Sweat Your Prayers, Movement as Spiritual Practice* and *Connections, The Five Threads of Intuitive Wisdom.*

CHAPTER 9

9. Housden, Roger, *Ten Poems to Change Your Life Again and Again.* New York: Harmony Books, 2007

This *Ten Poem Series*, now with five titles, selects very accessible, beautiful poems and follows them with short essays. They are a source of great wisdom and are exquisitely written. These books, along with his two anthologies *Risking Everything* and *Dancing with Joy*, provide a valuable entree into the poetic tradition.

Index by Title

Permission

Excerpts from "Kindness" by permission of the author, Naomi Shihab Nye, reprinted from *Words Under the Words*, 2009

About the Author

Bill E. Goldberg is a licensed Marriage and Family Therapist who shares here the essence of the life philosophy he developed over a twenty-year period as a counselor, writer, and teacher. A central focus of his work is to facilitate movement in the lives of his clients. His approach is informed by the wisdom and beauty of nature and follows the adage, "The river that continues flowing is the river that remains clean." To stimulate movement, he uses various modalities including the creative arts, *Voice Dialogue*, and emotional release techniques.

In addition to counseling, Bill has an extensive background in education, having taught at the college and university levels. He is a Certified Seminar Leader and has conducted seminars for businesses and other organizations teaching relaxation, communication, and self-assertion skills. His presentations have included seminars at Control Data Corporation, McDonnell Douglas Aircraft, Kaiser Permanente, Litton Computer Services, and The Learning Annex. Bill is the founder of Catch the Current Publishing whose mission is to assist people in creating more fulfilled, authentic, integrated lives. He is the producer of the CD, *Protecting the Diamond, Communication Skills to Create and Maintain Intimacy in Your Life.* Bill is also the author of three poetry books: *Catch the Current, Be Like the River,* and *The Journey.* He lives in Southern California and is available for counseling (in-person or on the phone), seminars, and poetry readings. He welcomes your comments about *The "And" Principle.* You can contact him at:

bill@catchthecurrentpublishing.com

"An important contribution to the art of intimacy."
— John Bradshaw, Author of *Homecoming* and *Bradshaw On: The Family*

It feels so good to be close to someone.
Protecting the Diamond shows you how to
create and maintain this feeling.

You Will Learn About:

- Two ways of living and communicating: one based on emotional injury and one based on emotional nurturance;
- Why self-esteem is the hub of the wheel of life and what allows us to live and communicate effectively;
- Understanding and developing compassion for our limitations;
- A four-part formula for resolving conflicts and problems;
- "I Messages," "You Messages," and how to communicate safely; and more.

To order a CD, visit www.catchthecurrentpublishing.com or send $15.95, plus $5.00 for shipping and handling, made payable to:

Catch the Current Publishing
P.O. Box 1685
Santa Monica, CA 90406-1685

(The CD is 70 minutes long and ends with poetry accompanied by music.)

CPSIA information can be obtained
at www.ICGtesting.com
Printed in the USA
LVHW042358300420
654814LV00003B/711

9 780966 146165